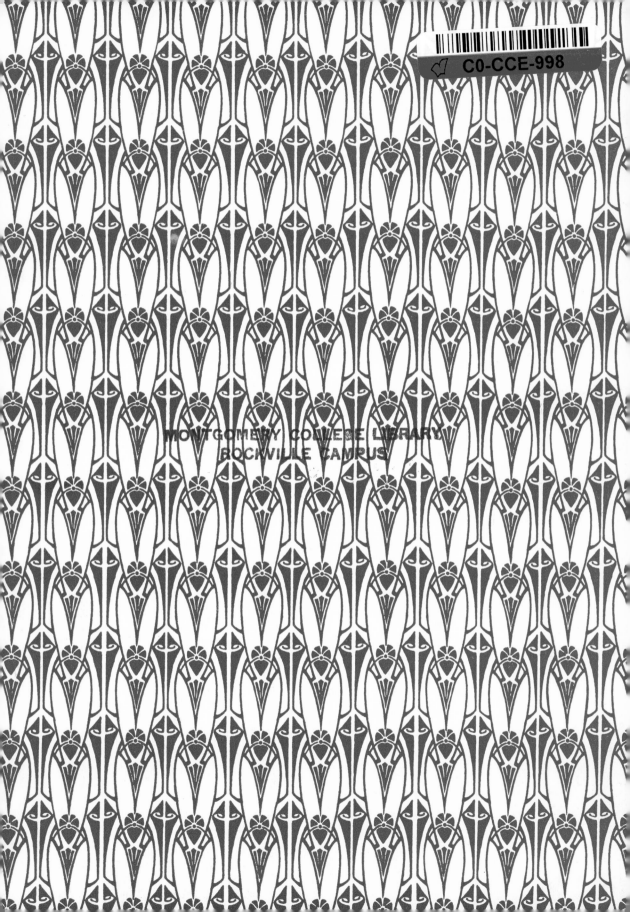

Letters
from
Rupert Brooke
to his publisher
1911–1914

From a photograph by Sherril Schell   Emery Walker Ph.sc.

Rupert Brooke

1913

London. Published by Emery Walker Limited. 16 Clifford's Inn. Fleet St. EC. May 1st 1916

LETTERS
from
RUPERT BROOKE
to his publisher
1911–1914

OCTAGON BOOKS
A division of Farrar, Straus and Giroux
New York, 1975

In memory of
Henry Lewis Batterman, Jr.
from his collection
of the original manuscripts
presently owned by his niece
Edith Scott Lynch.

Introduction

THE LETTERS OF RUPERT BROOKE were published in May 1968 under my editorship by Messrs. Faber and Faber. There had been a long period of incubation while letters were being collected from the various correspondents and differences of opinion as to what was suitable for publication were being resolved. Ultimately a well balanced collection was made public, though one small category was represented by only a single letter, namely Brooke's exchanges with the publisher of his first book, the only one to appear during his lifetime. This was the *Poems* of 1911, launched on 4 December by the small publishing firm of Sidgwick and Jackson in an edition of five hundred copies bound in black cloth boards with a printed label on the spine, priced at 2s.6d.

Efforts had of course been made to recover Brooke's letters to his publisher, Frank Sidgwick, but it was too late, the firm having sold them some years before. They had been absorbed into a private collection somewhere in the United States of America and could not be traced. A typewritten copy of the letter dated 20 September 1911 had been preserved and with this we had to be content. Mrs. Edith Lynch, niece of the collector who had acquired all the twenty-one letters concerned with the book has now come forward and has asked the Rupert Brooke Trustees to allow them to be printed in the present volume together with a few other manuscripts associated with them. This permission has been gladly given.

In May 1911 Brooke had established himself in the Old Vicarage, Grantchester, a short distance from Cambridge, in order to work on a dissertation in the hope of gaining a fellowship at King's College. The correspondence with Sidgwick began early in the next month. He had already been making efforts to find a publisher and in a letter[1] to a Cambridge friend, dated 11 January 1911, had remarked that he thought the publisher, J. M. Dent, would bring out his poems in about six months' time, but this hope came to nothing and some fresh line of attack had to be found. It is conjectured that contact with Frank Sidgwick, founder of the firm of Sidgwick and Jackson, was made through a common friend, Lytton Strachey. Sidgwick was himself an Old Rugbeian and so likely to be sympathetic to a proposal to publish the work of a young poet from his old school.

Brooke was already accustomed to seeing his poems in print, having made many contributions to Rugby School journals, to the *Westminster Gazette*, from which he had won a number of small prizes, to Cambridge magazines and to some London journals. Nevertheless the prospect of seeing a whole volume of his own work was as exciting to Brooke as to any other young poet. The publisher's first reaction followed the usual cautionary line – "hardly any poetry pays its way", "it is very difficult for us to take the risk of such a volume", although then revealing that his estimate of the cost of producing a volume of poems, which he regarded as "all worth publishing", would be about nine pounds. In fact it worked out at £9.17.6, not a very serious risk, one would have thought, even in 1911. Brooke, however, modestly took the point and agreed that the book should be published "on commission", himself paying the whole cost and giving Sidgwick a commission of fifteen per cent on all sales. He then proceeded to show that, although a poet, he had a hard business head and was determined to have his own way as to which poems were to be included, wishing to print a few unpleasant passages, such as 'The Sea-sick Lover', afterwards called 'The Channel Passage', 'Dawn', describing a night journey in a German train, and one to which he had given the title 'Lust'. These were to demonstrate that he was not addicted to 'prettiness' and could speak with a modern and explicit tongue. He enquired carefully about how much he was to put into advertising, how many free copies he was to receive, and, very sensibly, about typographical details, a subject of which publishers like to suppose that their clients know very little and with which they should not presume to meddle.

LUST

~~LIBIDO~~

How should I know ? The enormous wheels of will
  Drove me cold-eyed on tired and sleepless feet.
Night was void arms and you a phantom still,
  And day your far light swaying down the street.
As never fool for love, I starved for you ;
  My throat was dry and my eyes hot to see.
Your mouth so lying was most heaven in view,
  And your remembered smell most agony.

Love wakens love ! I felt your hot wrist shiver
  And suddenly the mad victory I planned
    Flashed real, in your burning bending head. . . .
My conqueror's blood was cool as a deep river
  In shadow ; and my heart beneath your hand
  Quieter than a dead man on a bed.

The subject on which Brooke and Sidgwick had a serious disagreement was the title 'Lust'. A compromise was reached by hiding the offensive word under the obscurity of a dead language, calling it 'Libido'. Brooke remained indignant at Sidgwick's prudery and altered the title by hand to 'Lust' in some copies given to his friends. An example of this is reproduced here from a proof-sheet given to J. C. Squire. Brooke continually demanded typographical changes, though apologising for seeming to be "unusually meticulous". He reacted, too, to the "impetuosity" of the printers, who were not carrying out his wishes, pretending to fear that they might suddenly bind his book in pink cloth when he wanted to have black.

In spite of all his care there were occasional misprints. Writing to a friend (Sybil Pye) on 22 December 1911, he asked "When you see copies of my book, will you surreptitiously change 'greasy' to 'queasy' (p. 35 last line), insert 'so' before 'fair', p. 32, and write LUST for LIBIDO, p. 34? The first is a misprint; the last is a sacrifice to my publisher's pudency. Other mistakes you may have spotted".[2]

The *Agreement* with the publisher, reproduced here, lays down the conditions usual at the time; it was witnessed by Virginia Stephen (afterwards Woolf), who happened to be a guest at the Old Vicarage at the time.

The *Poems* were not widely reviewed and sales were at first slow. Brooke was naturally sensitive to the opinions of his friends. In a letter to Sir Edward Marsh, a frank critic, he wrote on 22 December: "Your letter gave me great joy. It was very good of you to write. I horribly feel that degrading ecstasy that I have always despised in parents whose shapeless offspring are praised for beauty. People are queer about my poems. Some that I know very well & have great *sympathie* with, don't like them. Some people seem to like them. Some like only the early ones – them considerably, but the others not at all. These rather sadden me. I hobnob vaguely with them over the promising verses of a young poet, called Rupert Brooke, who died in 1908. But I'm much more concerned with the living, who don't interest them. God! it's so cheering to find someone who likes the

MEMORANDUM OF AGREEMENT made this *Twelfth* day of *August* 1911
BETWEEN Rupert Brooke Esq, of The Old Vicarage, Grantchester,
Cambridge., hereinafter called the Author, his heirs, executors,
and assigns, of the one part, and Sidgwick & Jackson Limited, of
3 Adam Street, Adelphi, London, W.C., hereinafter called the Publishers, of the other part; WHEREBY it is agreed as follows:-

(1) The Author having supplied the Publishers with the M.S. of
his poems, the Publishers undertake at the Author's charge to print

R B an edition of ~~Eight~~ *five* hundred copies and bind and advertise the
same as required and publish the said work in the Author's behalf
and offer it for sale through the ordinary trade channels at the
published price of two shillings and sixpence net.

(2) The Publishers shall produce the said work in accordance
with the specimens and estimates submitted to and approved by the Au
Author, who undertakes to bear all costs of production in accordance with the Publishers' letters to him, together with the charges
for Author's corrections on the proofs.

(3) The Publishers shall render to the Author an account of the
sales of the said work, reckoning thirteen copies as twelve, and
shall pay over to him the net amounts derived therefrom as received
less their commission of fifteen per cent. on such amounts. Accounts
shall be rendered half-yearly as at June 30th and December 31st in
each year and shall be settled in cash within three months of the
said dates respectively.

(4) The Publishers shall include the said work in their lists
and catalogues free of further charge, but all costs of newspaper
advertising shall be borne by the Author and debited to his account;

R B but the sum so spent shall not exceed the sum of £ 3 *(three)* pounds
without written instructions from the Author.

(Agreement continued to Folio 2.)

Folio 2 of Agreement
    Between Rupert Brooke Esq and Sidgwick and Jackson Ltd.

(5) If after two years from the date of publication the demand
for the said work shall in the Publishers' opinion have ceased, they
shall be at liberty to return to the Author the unsold stock of
the work, and this agreement shall thereupon determine.

(6) The Author undertakes to keep the Publishers indemnified

against all actions claims and demands which may be brought against
or made upon them by reason of the said work containing or being
alleged to contain any libellous or other actionable matter or to
be an infringement of any right or rights belonging to any other
party.

(7) The Publishers shall be allowed six free copies of the said
work for their file and travellers' use, and five copies for the
Statutory Libraries gratis.

                        SIGNED.

In the presence of

Virginia Stephen
    29 Fitzroy Square
        London W.

modern stuff, & appreciates what one's at. You can't think how your remarks and liking thrilled me."[3]

On another occasion he was able to be flippant about his verses. Writing to Marsh on 25 February 1912 he reported: "Mrs. Cornford tried to engage me in a controversy over the poems – she and her school. They are known as the Heart-criers, because they believe all poetry ought to be short, simple, naïve & a cry from the heart: the sort of thing an inspired child might utter if it was in the habit of posing to its elders. They object to my poetry as unreal, affected, complex, 'literary', & full of long words. I'm rewriting English Literature on their lines. Do you think this is a fair rendering of Shakespeare's first twenty sonnets if Mrs. Cornford had had the doing of them?

> *Triolet*
> If you would only have a son,
>> William, the day would be a glad one.
> It *would* be nice for everyone,
> If you would only have a son.
> – And, William, what would you have done
>> If Lady Pembroke had't had one?
> If you would only have a son,
>> William, the day *would* be a glad one.

It seems to me to have got the kernel of the situation, & stripped away all unnecessary verbiage or conscious adornment."[4]

It was not until 3 April 1913 that Brooke discovered by enquiring at Harold Monro's Poetry Bookshop in London that his book was out of print. He immediately wrote to Sidgwick asking about a reprint, thinking that it might already be under weigh – as, indeed, it was, a second edition being published in that month. He received his copies on 3 May. In September 1914 he was serving in the Naval Brigade and wrote to Sidgwick asking that the book should be reprinted as soon as the second edition was sold out. He remarked at the same time that his second volume of poems would have to wait

Sonnet

Not with vain tears, when we're beyond the sun,
    Will beat on the substantial doors, nor tread
    Those dusty high-roads of the aimless dead
Remembering Earth ; but rather Turn and run
Down some close-covered by-way of the air,
    Or low sweet alley between wind and wind,
    Stoop under faint gleams, thread the shadows, find
Some whispering ghost-forgotten nook ; and there

Spend in pure converse our eternal day ;
    Think each in each, immediately wise ;
Learn all we lacked before ; hear, know, and say
    What this tumultuous body now denies ;
And feel, who have laid our groping hands away ;
And see, no longer blinded by our eyes.

                                        Rupert Brooke

June 16ᵗʰ 1914

until the war was over, but, tragically, he died of septicaemia on a hospital ship in the Aegean on 23 April 1915, and could not see the second volume, *1914 and Other Poems*, prepared by his literary executor, Sir Edward Marsh, and published in June 1915.

Meanwhile the circumstances of his death and the fame of his War Sonnets had awakened a wide interest in his poetry, and the 1911 *Poems* were reprinted six times in 1915 and four times more up to July 1916. Nearly 99,000 copies had been distributed by May 1932. The poems were included in 1918 in Marsh's edition of the *Collected Poems*, with a memoir, and again in my edition of The *Poetical Works* of 1946. Both of these volumes have been sold in very large numbers and several thousand copies are still demanded every year, even though nearly sixty years have passed since Brooke's death. The publication of these letters for Mrs. Lynch provides welcome details of an important episode in English literary history.

Brooke's last letter to Sidgwick (included in the collected *Letters*, pages 626-7) was dated 23 October 1914, but was unconnected with his own work. He wished to suggest the publication of a volume of German caricatures of Prussian militarism taken from a periodical called *Simplicissimus*, as anti-Prussian propaganda, but the project was not thought to be practicable.

The late Mr. Henry Lewis Batterman, Jr.'s collection contains, among other Brooke manuscripts, a version of the sonnet, 'Not with vain tears', first printed in *New Numbers*, number 1, February 1914; this is reproduced here in facsimile. A fair copy, also in Brooke's hand, is among the manuscripts preserved in King's College, Cambridge. It is included among the *Poetical Works*.

GEOFFREY KEYNES

Notes:
[1] *The Letters of Rupert Brooke*, ed. Sir Geoffrey Keynes (London, Faber and Faber; New York, Harcourt, Brace and World, 1968), p. 271.
[2] *The Letters of Rupert Brooke*, p. 326.
[3] *The Letters of Rupert Brooke*, p. 327.
[4] *The Letters of Rupert Brooke*, p. 361.

Acknowledgements

As Sir Geoffrey states in The Introduction and in his 1954 *Bibliography of Rupert Brooke*: "Brooke's earlier letters to his publisher have been lost to sight since their owner sold them". That was more than 40 years ago. My uncle, in whose collection they were, and who was a great admirer of Brooke, was writing his bibliography when he died at a young age in 1939. He left me the legacy of his library and his enthusiasm for Brooke's work. Because of my deep affection for him and a desire to perpetuate his memory at some point and in some way, it seemed most natural to fill this gap and publish these letters.

My daughter, Elise, spurred me on to action by encouraging me to follow up an introduction to Miss Cathleen Nesbitt which had been arranged for me by Marjorie and Sherman Ewing and Suzanne and Samuel Taylor. Miss Nesbitt, a devoted friend and admirer of Brooke, was visiting New York in a play in the summer of 1973. Thanks to her, we learned how to go about publishing somebody else's work, and from that meeting stemmed many others. All of the fascinating people I met were each in their way extraordinarily helpful to the project and merit most sincere thanks.

First of all there is Sir Geoffrey Keynes, without whose generous help and guidance this collection would never have emerged. He suggested I contact The Morgan Library, where I received the invaluable assistance and editorial help of Herbert Cahoon, Curator of Library Manuscripts, and Director of Library Services. An old friend, George W. Martin, Jr., author and lawyer, was most wonderfully helpful in numerous ways, not the least of which was putting me in touch with Robert Nikirk, Librarian of The Grolier Club. Yet another good friend, Burchenal Ault, Vice-President of St. John's College, Santa Fe, and a director of Farrar, Straus and Giroux, Inc., sent me to that firm, whose subsidiary, Octagon Books, will distribute this volume. Through Roger Straus, the President of the firm, and Gordon Ray, President of The Guggenheim Foundation, I was put in touch with Dr. Lola Szladits, Curator of The Berg Collection at the New York Public Library, who was most helpful. To all of them my deep gratitude.

I wish to express thanks to the Rupert Brooke Trustees for their permission to publish this missing link as well as to the present firm of Sidgwick & Jackson Ltd. It has also been rewarding to work with David Godine's publishing firm, which was another suggestion of Sir Geoffrey. Bringing these letters to publication has been a most fruitful and educational experience, and is, I think, a fitting tribute to my uncle's memory.

EDITH SCOTT LYNCH
February 17, 1975

The Letters

1 🌼 *June 12, 1911*

The Old Vicarage
Grantchester
Cambridge
Monday June 12
1911

Dear Mr. Sidgwick,

I want to publish a volume of poems: I should like to publish them with you, rather than anywhere else, if it's possible. There are some fifty of them, forty-odd ready and the rest being finished. Some have appeared in The English Review, The Nation, The Westminster Gazette, and other places. I think they'd sell well enough in Cambridge and one or two other places to avoid a loss; but I'd take the risk of that, if you thought it risky. Anyhow, we could discuss that sort of arrangement if you thought them worth publishing. I shall be in London on Wednesday morning: and again, on Friday. If you thought it worth doing, could you see me, any time? I'll bring the volume to your offices on Wednesday morning. Could you, if you get this on time, have a note or message there for me?

Yours sincerely
Rupert Brooke

Monday June 12
1911

Dear Mrs Sidgwick,

I want to publish a volume of
poems: I should like to publish
them with you, rather than anywhere
else, if it's possible. There are
some fifty of them, forty-odd ready,
and the rest being finished.
Some have appeared in The English
Review, The Nation, The Westminster
Gazette, and other places. I
think they'd sell well enough in
Cambridge and one or two other
places to avoid a loss; but
I'd take the risk of that, if
you thought it risky. Anyhow,
we could discuss that sort of
arrangement if you thought them
worth publishing. I shall be
in London on Wednesday morning: and
again on Friday. If you thought
it worth doing, could you see me,
any time? I'll bring the
volume to your offices on Wednesday

morning.   Could you, if you
get this in time, leave a
note or message there for
me?

   yours sincerely

      Rupert Brooke

The Old Vicarage
Grantchester
Cambridge
July 16
1911

Dear Mr. Sidgwick,

Thanks for your letter; and for proposing to print the poems.

I should think your suggestion of issuing them on commission for me is quite a good one. I can afford ten pounds or so.

I have four more poems finished, and about five which I shall soon have finished, all of which I want, if they turn out well, to put in the book. I could have them done in ten days or a fortnight. When the book is being made, I want to have the proofs some fairly long period for reflection. So I should like to know when you think it ought to be published and how long the various stages take.

I am going to be in London this week, I think, on Thursday, Friday, & Saturday morning. It might save time if I could talk over various arrangements? I should like to see rough estimates of the cost of a small edition. The additional poems will be, say, nine, averaging 25 lines. I might leave out one or two of the older ones, which aren't very good. Personally I don't care much for the "Babylon" one. And I should be very sorry to leave out the "Sea-sickness" sonnet. But we might talk about that too. I have no very definite ideas about the get-up, yet.

Yours truly
Rupert Brooke

The Old Vicarage   July 16
    Grantchester   ————
        Cambridge   1911

Dear Mr Sidgwick,

        Thanks for your letter; and for proposing
to print the poems.

I should think your suggestion of issuing them on
commission for me is quite a good one. I
can afford ten pounds or so.

I have four more poems finished, and
about five which I ~~shall~~ shall soon have
finished, all of which I want, if
they turn out well, to put in the
book. I could have them done in
ten days or a fortnight.
                                                      While
the book is being made, I want to
have the proofs some ~~the~~ fairly long
period for reflection.   So I
should like to know when you
think it ought to be published
and how long the various stages take.

I am going to be in London this week, I
think, on Thursday, Friday, + Saturday morning.
It might save time if I could
talk over various arrangements? I

should like to see rough estimates
of the cost of a small edition. The
additional poems will be, say, nine,
averaging 25 lines. I might leave
out one or two of the older ones, which
aren't very good. Personally
I don't care much for the "Babylon"
one. And I should be very sorry
to leave out the "Seasickness" sonnet.
But we might talk about that too.
I have no very definite ideas about the
get-up, yet. —

Yours truly

Rupert Brooke

The Old Vicarage
Grantchester
Cambridge
August 6th 1911

Dear Sidgwick,

Thanks for the Estimate, Agreement, & Letter.

Estimate: I hadn't realized when you mentioned ten pounds that advertising, binding, and corrections would pull it up so much. However, it doesn't matter. But could you let me know quite roughly what *ad valorem* is likely to come – about what the average for a book of poems of this size, with an ordinary amount of correction, is? As for binding, I suppose you only bind part of the issue first, and the rest if the first lot look likely to sell out? How many will be bound at first? What, I mean, will be the *initial* cost for binding – for *200*? or *250*?

Letter: I agree it'll be better to print *500*. And let's compromise on *The Channel Passage* being "hidden away," either at the end or, where it might be still more untrackable, in the middle.

Agreement: It looks all right. But there are one or two points I want enlightening about. (1) What about review copies? I suppose you see about sending them out, etc. But do they count in the sales? I suppose anyhow up to a certain number go free? Also *Presentation Copies.* (2) What about copyright? I don't know the law. I suppose *I* get it all right?

You know best about the amount for advertising; so I agree to £3 as you advise.

You promised to let me have the MSS back to be looking over. I'm working at the new stuff. But I want the other to do when I'm too tired for writing. Can it be sent, here?

I'm sending back the agreement, in case there's anything to be added with regard to those two points. If it's all right, I'm willing to sign.

Yours
Rupert Brooke

August 6th 1911

The Old Vicarage
Grantchester
Cambridge

Dear Sidgwick,

Thanks for the Estimate, Agreement, & Letter.

Estimate —

I hadn't realised, when you mentioned ten pounds, that advertising, binding, & corrections would pull it up so much. However, it doesn't matter. But could you let me know — what quite roughly what ad valorem is likely to come — about what the average for a book of poems of this size, with an ordinary amount of correction, is? As for binding, I suppose you only bind part of the issue first, and the rest if the first lot look likely to sell out? How many will be bound at first? What I mean, will be the initial cost for binding — for 200? or 250?

Letter.

I agree it'll be better to print 500. And let's compromise on The Channel Passage being "hidden away," either at the end or, where it might be still more untrackable, in the middle.

Agreement.

It looks all right. But there are one or two points I want enlightening about. (1) What about review copies? I suppose you see about sending them out, etc. But do they count in the sales? I suppose anyhow up to a certain number go free? Also Presentation Copies

2)

6. VIII. 11.

(2) What about Copyright? I don't know
the law. Suppose I get it
all right?

You know best about the amount for
advertising; so I will agree to £3 as
you advise.

You promised to let me have the
M.S.S. back to be looking over. I'm
working at the new stuff. But I
want the other to do when I'm
too tired for writing. Can
it be sent here?

I'm sending back the agreement, in case
there's anything to be added with regard
to those two points. If it's
all right I'm willing to sign

yours
Rupert Brooke

4 *August 11, 1911*

> The Old Vicarage
> Grantchester
> Cambridge
> Friday

Thanks for MSS and letter. I will sign agreement if you will send it.

> *Rupert Brooke*

---

5 *August 21, 1911*

> LITTLE TALLAND HOUSE
> FIRLE, LEWES,
> SUSSEX.
> Monday August 21

Dear Sidgwick,

Here is the agreement, duly witnessed. Many thanks. I'm sorry I've not finished the poems. I've been toiling at them, with less success than one can well imagine. But at length I do seem within sight of the end. Can I have a week to finish them? I think that ought to do it.

> Yours
> *Rupert Brooke*

The Old Vicarage
Grantchester
Wednesday
Sept 20
1911

Dear Sidgwick,

Is the objection to "Lust" only that it's bad as poetry or also that it's shocking as morals? I can't see that it's any worse as poetry than the rest of the book (except one or two poems). Technically it's not much, I admit; but any fool can write a technically good sonnet. And I hope that the new-ness of the idea might counterbalance that.

If it's thought to be improper, it must be sadly misunderstood. Its meaning is quite "proper" and so moral as to be almost untrue. If the title's too startling *Libido* or Ἐπιθυμία could be substituted: though I'm afraid that would only make it more obscure.

My own feeling is that to remove it would be to overbalance the book still more in the direction of unimportant prettiness. There's plenty of that sort of work in the other pages for the readers who like it. They needn't read the parts which are new and serious. About a lot of the book, I occasionally feel like Ophelia – that I've turned "thought and affliction, passion, hell itself, – to favour and to prettiness." So I'm extra keen about the places where I think that thought and passion, are, however clumsily, *not* so transmuted. This was one of them. It seemed to have qualities of reality & novelty that made up for the clumsiness. The expression is only good in places. But the idea seemed to me important and moving.

I know a lot of people who like my earlier work better than

my present. They will barely notice this sonnet. There are others who prefer my present stuff. I've shown the sonnet to some of them. They thought it good (by my standards, whatever they may be!) – And they weren't, I assure you, – though they were of all ages and kinds – shocked.

I should like it to stand, as a representative in the book, of abortive poetry against literary verse; and because I can't see any aesthetic ground against it which would not damn three quarters of the rest of the book too, or any moral ground at all. If your reader has misunderstood the sonnet I will explain it to him. If you really think it finally ruins the chances of the book, I suppose it ought to go. If you think it will only decrease the sales, we could make some additional agreement about the number sold within a year, or something. If it's too near the beginning, it can be buried.

Yours

Rupert Brooke

I should like to know if the acknowledgement at the beginning is all right.

I can come to London (preferably Thursdays, or Saturdays) if there's anything that needs discussion.

The Old Vicarage   Wednesday
Grantchester   Sept 20
                                                        1911

Dear Sidgwick,

1. Is the objection to "Lust" only that it's bad as poetry or also that it's shocking as morals? I can't see that it's any worse as poetry than the rest of the book (except one or two poems). Technically it's not much, I admit; but any fool can write a technically good sonnet. And I hoped that the new-ness of the idea ~~~~ might counterbalance that.

If it's thought to be improper, it must be sadly misunderstood. Its meaning is quite "proper" and so moral as to be almost untrue. If the title's too startling Libido or Ἐπιθυμία could be substituted: Though I'm afraid that would only make it more obscure.

[My own feeling is that to remove it would be to overbalance the book still more in the unimportant direction of prettiness. There's plenty of that out of work in the other pages for the reader who like it. They needn't read the parts which are new and serious. About a lot of the book I occasionally feel like Ophelia: that I've turned "Thought and affliction, passion, hell itself, — — to favour and to prettiness." So I'm extra keen about the places where I think that thought and passion, are, however clumsily, not so transmuted. This was

one of them. It seemed to have qualities of
reality + novelty that made up for the
clumsiness. The expression is only good in
places. † But the idea seemed to me important
and moving. I know a lot of people
who like my earlier work better than my
present. They will barely notice this sonnet.
There are others who prefer my present stuff. I've
shown the sonnet to some of them. They
thought it good (by my standards, whatever
they may be!)— And they weren't, I assure
you, — though they were of all ages and
kinds — shocked.

[I should like it to stand, as a representative in
the book, of abortive poetry against literary verse;
and because I can't see any aesthetic
ground against it which would not damn three quarters
of the rest of the book too, or any moral
ground at all.] If your reader
has misunderstood the sonnet I will explain it
to him. If you really think it finally
mars the chances of the book, I suppose it ought
to go. If you think it will only
decrease the sales we could make some
additional agreement that about the
number sold within a year, or something.
If it's too near the beginning, it can be buried.

yours Rupert Brooke

I should like to know if the acknowledgement at the beginning is
all right.
I can come to London (preferably Thursdays or Saturdays) if there is
anything that needs discussion.

The Old Vicarage
Grantchester
Cambridge
September 28 1911

Dear Sidgwick,

(a) Thanks for your first letter. I'm glad the poem's going to appear. I rather think Ἐπιθυμία is a better translation of the English title than *Libido*: but perhaps the Greek would be a nuisance? We might write *Epithumia*.

I wrote the prefatory note in that form because I did not want to say where they'd appeared. I now think it does not matter, so I will rewrite it; the more that in giving leave the editors seem very anxious I should say *which* poems they godfathered. Actually though, the copyright's mine; isn't it?

(b) Thanks for this proof. I like it. There is one thing I feel very strongly about, and that is that each line (especially in sonnets) should be one line. At present two are broken. About the position of the titles I am not sure. I *think* I prefer them at the side: but I should like to *see* one in the middle: unless you think it wouldn't do. I feel a little dim and amateurish about the appearance of a book. Can I therefore have a proof of this page (p.1) with the eighth and ninth lines of the sonnet printed as one line each instead of two, on the same sized page. And can I *also* have a proof on a slightly larger page, if the line then becomes too long to look well on this page? If any more is set up, I should like to see a page with a *longer* poem on it; it's hard to judge on a sonnet, in some points.

Other points: I do not like the very large initial letter. Can it be an ordinary capital? And if you're sending two proofs, can the title of one be in the centre, of the other at the side, as now, but in large *italics*? I want to see how that looks.

If I can see these things, or as many as are possible, I will decide. I am sorry if I am unusually meticulous.

I expect to be in town a day next week.

Yours truly
Rupert Brooke

The Old Vicarage
Grantchester
Cambridge

September 28 '14

Dear Sidgwick,

(a) Thanks for your first letter. I'm glad the poems is going to appear. I rather think ~~Epithymia~~ is a better translation of the English title than Libido : but perhaps the Greek would be a nuisance? We might write Epithumia.

I wrote the prefatory note in that form because I did not want to say where they'd appeared. I now think it does not ~~both~~ matter, so I will rewrite it; the more that in giving leave the editors seem very anxious I should say which poems they god fathered. Actually, though, the copyright's mine; is it it?

(b) Thanks for this proof. I like it. ~~Parts~~ There is one thing I feel very strongly about, and that is that each line (especially in sonnets) should be one line. At present two are broken. ~~Could you~~ About the position of the titles I am not sure. I think I prefer them at the side : but I should like to see one in the middle. — unless you think it wouldn't do. I feel a little dim and amateurish about the appearance of a book.

Can I therefore have a proof of this page ~~(£¼)~~ (£0.1) with the eighth and ninth lines of the sonnet printed as one line each instead of two, on the same sized page. And can I also have a proof on a slightly larger page, if the line then becomes too long to look well on this

page?   ⟨Other⟩   If any more is set up, ⟨I should⟩
like to see a page with a longer poem on it; it's
hard to judge on a sonnet, in some points.

Other points: I do not like the very large initial
letter.   Can it be an ordinary capital? ⟨...⟩   And
if you're sending two proofs, ⟨...⟩ can the title
of one be in the centre, of the other at the
side, as now, but in large *italics*?   I want to
see how that looks.

If I can see these things, or as many as are possible,
I will decide.
I am sorry ⟨to be⟩ if I am unusually meticulous.
I expect to be in town a day next week.

                        Yours truly
                                Rupert Brooke

Tuesday October 10 1911
24 Bilton Road
Rugby
Telephone no: Rugby 50

Dear Sidgwick,

I have corrected the proofs, and returned them. I like the general appearance of it all very much.

One or two points. *The English Review* & *Nation*, in giving leave to reprint, cautiously demanded that I should say *which* poems they godfathered. I don't know if I need: but I thought I'd humour them. So I have had to write out the whole page again. And I spell acknowledgement with several "e"s.

I suppose you have explained to the printers that (1) large initials, and (2) superfluous headlines are to go.

P. 47 eat or ate? if "eat" is possible, I want it. It may be a "solecism"?

As for Turning-over: I should like to know what the printers can and will do. There are sixteen decasyllabic sonnets. All are occasionally Turned-over now. I think it would be worth while doing anything to get them right. Certainly resetting just them to a wider measure.

If that is done it would be worth while to extend it to any of *Thoughts on the Shape. . .* , *Town and Country*, *Jealousy*, and *Second-Best* that can't be coaxed into neatness at present. But I think they all can, probably.

The same might also be worth while for the dodecasyllabic *Vision of the Arch Angels* & *Ante Aram*.

Single instances on pp. 7, 31, 38, 71, and 88 could probably be squeezed in without altering the measure.

All the rest can go.

You'll probably be able to tell me if this is possible, and easier than resetting the whole.

P. 24. They've printed the Long Title rather badly, haven't they? – as if it were central?

I suppose you've no proof with a few titles in the middle? I like it very much as it is: but I'm not certain I mightn't like it even more in the middle. Perhaps it's too late.

I'm here till Saturday: Grantchester for the week-end: then London next Monday afternoon, if there's anything to be said.

yrs

Rupert Brooke

---

9 🦪 *October 12, 1911*

24 Bilton Road
Rugby
Thursday October 12 1911

Dear Sidgwick,

I *do* want to see some revised proofs, for one or two other details besides the turn-over lines. I'll only keep them the inside of a day. And I do want to get the majority of those turn-overs right. The printers owe us some trouble, for being so damnably forthright. I hope their impetuosity won't bind it all in pink before more's said. I want black. Is it possible?

Yours

Rupert Brooke

10 🐚 *Received October 24, 1911*

21 Fitzroy Square
W.C.

Dear Sidgwick,

The *New Age* wants to print a column and a half of poems by me. They want them from the book, as I've no others and no time to do them. I haven't accepted the proposal, yet. I feel very little either way. But I thought possibly it might be a good advertisement: and I shouldn't go to the trouble of altering my *Acknowledgement*. But I thought I'd better ask you, as you would know if it was a good thing, and might have some objection. If you don't think it in any way undesirable, I think I shall do it.

I wonder when there'll be any Review Proofs for me to see?

Yours
Rupert Brooke

---

11 🐚 *October 25, 1911*

21 Fitzroy Square
Tuesday

Dear Sidgwick

I think of letting them have *The Fish* p. 12, *The Life Beyond* p. 23, and, if they wanted more, either *Libido* p. 33, or *Mummia* p. 10. Is that all right?

I suppose they ought to go in next week so as not to coincide too nearly with the book?

Rupert Brooke

12 ❧ *November 16, 1911*

76 Charlotte St.
Bloomsbury

Dear Sidgwick,

The *New Age*, having a principle against footnotes, has offered to print an advertisement *free*. I suppose it's worth accepting. Could you see to it, with the other advts?

Yrs
Rupert Brooke

13 ❧ *Between December 4 and 12th 1911*

TELEGRAPHIC ADDRESS C/O "ENELSEE, LONDON."

TELEPHONE NO.   NATIONAL LIBERAL CLUB,
3700 VICTORIA.   WHITEHALL PLACE, S.W.
4 LINES

76 Charlotte Street
Bloomsbury, W.

Dear Sidgwick,

I was so overwhelmed by a final pressure of work against time that I had no time to acknowledge the books. I thought the whole appearance of them very good and exactly what I wanted, print, binding and all. Many thanks.

I don't know how many complimentary copies it's usual to have but—complimentary or not—I want *six* more, four ordinary and two *unbound* (for friends who are going to bind them in gold and diamonds and vellum). May I have them? Or ought I to order them otherhow?

The King's man who reviewed me for the Morning Post is —I have long known—an imbecile.

Yours,
Rupert Brooke

TELEPHONE NO.
3700 VICTORIA.
4 LINES.

NATIONAL LIBERAL CLUB,
WHITEHALL PLACE, S.W.

TELEGRAPHIC ADDRESS, ℅ "ENELSEE, LONDON."

Date — between Dec. 4 and 12th 1911

76, Charlotte Street
Bloomsbury. W.

Dear Sidgwick,

I was so overwhelmed
by a final poring
of work again
this That I
had no time to
acknowledge the he
books. I thought

24 Bilton Road
Rugby
Monday
Jan 8, 1912.

Dear Sidgwick,

My book has not been mentioned in the *Books Received* in *The Times 4 Dec.* Literary Supplement – the bit which professes to register all books sent for review. I hope the *Times* copy hasn't gone astray in any way?

If you send a review copy to the *Middleborough Gazette* (which has a vast circulation in the North, & a taste for literature) & mark it *P. J. Reid* (an editor I know): it will probably get a good review.

I am going abroad in a day or two – perhaps for some months. I suppose there'll be no likelihood of a second edition in the visible future? For if there is I'd like a chance of correcting five or six irritating misprints.

Yours
Rupert Brooke

24 Bilton Road
Rugby
Monday
Jan 8. 1911 [?1912]

Dear Sidgwick,

My book has not been advertised in the Books in the Times since 4 Dec.

Literary Supplement — the list which proposes to strike all books sent for review. I hope that the Times copy hasn't gone astray in any way? If you send a review

cops to the Midsborough Gazette (which has a vast circulation in the North, + a taste for literature) + mark it P.J. Reid (an edition I know): it will probably get a good review.

I am going abroad in a day or two — perhaps for some months — for which there will be no support (italthous) of a decent edition... in the villages perhaps 2 for reviews

if there is I'd like a chance of
correcting five or six irritating misprints

yours ever

Rupert Brooke

Hotel du Pavillon
Cannes
(temporarily)
16. 1. 12.

Dear Sidgwick,

Many thanks. The corrections I have noted are these:

p. viii. DAY THAT I HAVE LOVED   E/

p. 35. last line. "greasy" to be changed to "queasy"

p. 32. second line of sestet: insert "so" between "was" and "fair".

p. 81. line 8. "Gtae" to be changed to "Gate".

I think that is all.

The reason I mentioned *The Times* was that people keep telling me the book isn't out, because it hasn't been listed in the Supplement. Could you send them a card to reprimand them? or, if it's my business, I will.

Yours
Rupert Brooke

16 ❧ *August 29, 1912*

24 Bilton Road
Rugby
29. 8. 12.

Last week you advertised in the Times Literary Supplement, & spelt my name wrong. Please spell it right.

Rupert Brook E

POST CARD

Sidgwick and Jackson
4 Adam Street
Adelphi

London —

24 Bilton Road
Rugby

29. 8. 12.

Last week you advertised
in the Times Literary Supplement,
& spelt my name wrong.
Please spell it right.

Rupert Brooke.

17 ❦ *September 28, 1912*

24 Bilton Road
Rugby
September 28, 1912

Dear Sidgwick,

(1) The accounts which were more or less promised for the end of July, haven't reached me yet.

(2) Eddie Marsh (I don't know if you know him) is planning a book called "Georgian Poets" – containing the work of some ten moderns. It is designed to persuade people at large that a lot of good stuff is being written. It is only to include stuff published in the last two years. It is to come out by Christmas. He has already got W. W. Gibson, Lascelles Abercrombie, & John Drinkwater to consent. He's trying Masefield & Davies & some others. He wants to print, of *mine*, *Dust*, *The Fish*, *Town & Country*, & *Dining-room Tea*; & a later poem written this summer. I have consented. I suppose you won't have any objections? It seems to me it can be nothing but a good advertisement. If there are any profits, I gather he's going to divide them up amongst the authors. And he'll make "the usual acknowledgements."

I hope you're well. I go out walks with your old housemaster twice a week, & hear the moderns condemned.

Yours
Rupert Brooke

24 Bilton Road
Rugby

September 28. 1912

Dear Sidgwick,

(1.) The accounts which were more or less
promised for the end of July, haven't
reached me yet.

(2.) Eddie Marsh (I don't know if you know
him) is planning ~~to publish~~ a book called
"Georgian Poets" — containing the work
of some ten moderns. It is designed
to persuade people at large that a
lot of good ~~stuff~~ is being written. It is only
to include stuff ~~written~~ published in the last
two years. It is to come out by
Christmas. He has already got
W. W. Gibson, Lascelles Abercrombie, & John
Drinkwater to consent. He's trying Masefield
& Davies & some others. He wants to
print of mine, Dust, The Fish, Town & Country,
& Dining-room Tea ; & a later poem
written this summer.   I have

consented. I suppose you won't have any
objection? It seems to me it can
be nothing but a good advertisement. If
there are any profits, I gather he's going to
divide them up amongst the authors. And
he'll make "the usual acknowledgements."

I hope you're well. I go out
walks with your old housemaster
thrice a week, & hear the moderns
condemned —

Yours
Rupert Brooke

[bei Herrn Dudley Ward
Berlin
Charlottenburg
Berlinerstrasse 100]
24 Bilton Road
Rugby
17. 11. 12.

Dear Sidgwick,

In June you promised me my accounts by the end of July. I waited weekly till sometime in September, and then reminded you again. You said they'd very soon be ready. It's now half-way through November. I wish you'd let me have them as soon as possible.

You said the copyright of my poems was mine: so I gave leave to Marsh to reprint four in his *Georgian Poets*, and "Q". to print two (or three) in the *Oxford Book of Victorian Verse*. But perhaps I told you. I suppose it's all right?

Yours truly
Rupert Brooke

19 🦪 *April 3, 1913*

TELEGRAPHIC ADDRESS C/O "ENELSEE, LONDON."
TELEPHONE NO.   NATIONAL LIBERAL CLUB,
3700 VICTORIA.   WHITEHALL PLACE, S.W.
4 LINES

> c/o E. Marsh
> 5 Raymond Buildings
> Gray's Inn
> W.C.
> Thursday
> April 3

Dear Sidgwick,

If as the Poetry Bookshop people report, my book is sold out, I suppose you've got a second edition under weigh.

In any case, when it *is* ready, can you send me three copies, to Bilton Road Rugby. I want to give some away, & want to give unmisprinted ones, rather than the old—

Shall I get my December accounts soon?

> Yours sincerely,
> *Rupert Brooke*

20 🐚 *April 16, 1913*

5 Thurloe Square
South Kensington
April 16, 1913

Dear Sidgwick,

If the three copies of my new impression, that I asked for, have already gone to Rugby, well & good. But if not, can they be sent to me at this address?

Yours sincerely
Rupert Brooke

---

21 🐚 *May 3, 1913*

5, THURLOE SQUARE, S.W.
TEL. 6531 WESTERN.

May 3, 1913

Dear Sidgwick,

The books arrived; many thanks. But shall I ever get my account up to the end of 1912? I'm going to America in a fortnight or so: & I want to clear things before then.

Yours sincerely
Rupert Brooke

22 ❦ *September 19, 1914*

c/o E. Marsh

5, RAYMOND BUILDINGS,

GRAY'S INN.

Sept 19. 1914.

Dear Sidgwick,

I have obtained a commission in the R. Naval Brigade, & am going into Camp for sometime, then abroad. If ever people start buying poetry again, & my second impression sells out, please start a third.

My next volume, of course, will have to wait till the war's over.

I have had no accounts for my poems for a long time. Could you make some up & send me them?

Yours sincerely

Rupert Brooke

C/o E. Marsh
5, Raymond Buildings.
Gray's Inn.

Sept 19. 1914.

Dear Sidgwick,

I have obtained a commission in the R. Naval Brigade, I am going into camp for sometime, then abroad.

If ever people start buying poetry again, + my second edition sells out, please start a third.

My next volume, of course, will have to wait till the war's over.

I have had no accounts for my poems for a long time. Could you make some up + send me them?

Yours ever

Rupert Brooke

Anson Battalion
Second Naval Brigade
Betteshanger
Eastry
October 23
1914

Dear Sidgwick,

I've had an idea — in the intervals of picnics at Antwerp, etc. It occurred to me & to a friend of mine. So other people *may* be thinking of acting on it.

It's this. I've lived long enough in Germany to know how extraordinarily good & pungent criticism of things Prussian *Simplicissimus* contains. I suggest a selection from *Simplicissimus* caricatures, since, say, 1900, under four or five heads — the Army, the Royal Family, Bureaucracy, the Prussian — some sixty of them: the whole to be called, *"What Germany thinks of Germany"* or some such title. There are several places one can get the *Simplicissimus.* And it really *does* give the evil & ridiculous side of what we're fighting against, better than anyone else.

I wish I were at leisure sufficiently to ask if you'd let me prepare such a book. But I'm afraid I'm not, at present. But there must be a lot of people competent. I think it's a book that *should* be published; & I think it would be a vast success.

Yours

Rupert Brooke

October 23
1914

Anson Battalion
Second Naval Brigade
Betteshanger
Eastry

Dear Sidgwick,

I've had an idea — in the interval of picnics at Antwerp, etc. — It occurred to me + to a friend of mine. So few people may see the (Punches) factory or it. 15 min. I've lived long enough in Germany to know has extraordinary good + pungent things satirization things Prussian Simplic —

— issimus contrain. I suggest a selection from Simplicissimus caricatures of things since, say, 1900, under four or five heads — the Army, the Royal Family, Bureaucracy, the Prussian, — some sixty of them — the whole to V them: "what Germany (or called) what Germany thinks of Germany" or some things of Germany. There are met with. several places one can get the Simplicissimus. And it really does give the evil + ridiculous side of what was fighting against, better than anyone else. I wish I were at leisure

sufficiently to ~~offer~~ ask if you'd let
me prepare such a book. But
I'm afraid I'm not, at present. But
there must be a lot of people competent.
~~And~~ I think it's a book that <u>should</u>
be published: & I think it would
be a vast success.

Yours

Rupert Brooke

This book has been printed in an edition of four hundred copies
for Edith Scott Lynch in March, 1975. The design is by Katy
Homans at The Godine Press. The type, Bell, was set by
Michael and Winifred Bixler. The paper is Mohawk
Superfine. The Meriden Gravure Company printed
the offset facsimiles, & the transcripts were printed
letterpress by Maria Epes at The Godine Press.
Of the edition, ten books, numbered I-X have
been bound by hand with Cockerel end-
papers by Arno Werner. The remainder
of the books, of which 340 are for distri-
bution by Farrar, Straus, & Giroux,
are numbered 11-400, & have been
bound by Robert Burlin & Sons.
This is copy number *240*

HENRY LEWIS BATTERMAN JR.